STAY

MR.

MRS.

AFTER YOU'RE

Mom & Dad

DAVID & CHRISTINE GIBSON

Stay Mr. & Mrs.
After You're
Mom & Dad

DAVID & CHRISTINE GIBSON

Liguori
ONE LIGUORI DRIVE
LIGUORI MO 63057-9999

Imprimi Potest:
Harry Grile, CSsR, Provincial
Denver Province, The Redemptorists

Published by Liguori Publications
Liguori, Missouri 63057

To order, call 800-325-9521
www.liguori.org

Cataloging-in-Publication Data on file with the Library of Congress

p ISBN: 978-0-7648-2187-5
e ISBN: 978-0-7648-2287-2

Liguori Publications, a nonprofit corporation, is an apostolate of The Redemptorists. To learn more about The Redemptorists, visit Redemptorists.com.

Printed in the United States of America
17 16 15 14 13 / 5 4 3 2 1
First Edition

Table of Contents

Introduction

Certainly [children] are a gift from the Lord,
the fruit of the womb, a reward.

Dear Parents-to-Be,

We are so very excited for you as you embark on this journey into parenthood, your life's true vocation. As the psalmist tells us, you are preparing to receive a gift from the Lord. God has selected you to raise and nurture one of his beloved children, and you will be forever changed by this calling. You will experience overwhelming joy upon seeing that beautiful face for the first time, tenth time, thousandth time. Your heart will swell with love and warmth when those little arms squeeze your neck tight. Your eyes may fill with tears and your heart may ache when you realize just how quickly that baby is growing and changing before your eyes. In short, you will love as you have never loved.

   In all corners of the world, parents-to-be are preparing for this exciting chapter of life. In our corner, that usually involves baby registries, showers, nursery decorating, childbirth classes, and endless shopping

7

trips. The nursery will be just the right color, the décor perfectly darling, and books and experts on childbirth and childcare consulted. With all of this preparation, baby's needs will undoubtedly be met. But what about your needs? What about your spouse's needs?

Research has long indicated that as much as we love, adore, and enjoy our children, the responsibilities and stress of child rearing can take their toll on a marriage. In fact, a graph of marital satisfaction over the course of a lifetime creates a U-shaped curve, with the dip occurring during the years of child rearing. With the majority of couples, conflict tends to increase, while positive interactions and affection decrease after baby. This is not welcome news to parents-to-be, but it is vital to realize the importance of focusing on marital issues while bringing up baby. Our marriage is precious and fundamental to us, to our children, and indeed to our world.

In the eyes of the Church, the importance of marriage and family cannot be overstated. The *Catechism of the Catholic Church* states that the family "should be called a *domestic church.* It is a community of faith, hope, and charity; it assumes singular importance in the Church…. The Christian family is a communion of persons, a sign and image of the communion of the Father and Son in the Holy Spirit" (*CCC* 2204–2205). When speaking to the clergy and the faithful on the role of the Christian family in the modern world *(Familiaris Consortio)*, Pope

John Paul II explained that parental love is to be for children a visible sign of God's love.

Given this awesome task of building the domestic church and actually becoming the sign of God's love for our children, we need to focus on maintaining a happy marriage as the foundation of a peaceful, Christ-centered home. Couples who make a point to nurture their marital relationship are providing for their children a model of what love and marriage should look like. These children enjoy a great feeling of peace, security, and stability as they grow, knowing that mom and dad love them and each other. In an uncertain and chaotic world, they can view their families as a haven, a refuge, truly "the visible sign of the very love of God."

We hope this workbook will prove helpful as you begin to build your domestic church. May God bless you and your family always.

With God's Peace,
David and Christine Gibson

1. Prayer

*Have no anxiety at all, but in everything,
by prayer and petition, with thanksgiving,
make your requests known to God.
Then, the peace of God that surpasses
all understanding will guard your hearts
and minds in Christ Jesus.*

PHILIPPIANS 4:6–7

This is a most exciting time in your marriage as you stand united, ready to cross the threshold from couplehood to family. It is a miraculous and momentous transition, and amid all of the excitement and preparation, we need to pause and reflect on what it means to become a family, and then to contemplate the role of prayer during this very special period of preparation.

The *Catechism* states, "The Christian family constitutes a specific revelation and realization of ecclesial communion, and for this reason it can and should be called a *domestic church*. It is a community of faith, hope, and charity"(*CCC* 2204).

As you embark on this adventure, this ministry, and this mission of building a domestic church, let's reflect on the role prayer must play in your preparation. Holy Scripture makes it clear that when Jesus faced important milestones in his ministry, he devoted himself to prayer to the Father:

- The night before he chose his Twelve Apostles, "he departed to the mountain to pray, and he spent the night in prayer to God"(Luke 6:12).

- At the time of the transfiguration, the Lord "took Peter, John, and James and went up the mountain to pray. While he was praying, his face changed in appearance"(Luke 9:28–29).

- On the eve of his passion and death, "Jesus came with them to a place called Gethsemane, and he said to his disciples, 'Sit here while I go over there and pray'" (Matthew 26:36).

If Jesus, the second Person of the Trinity, needed time and space to pray as he built the Church, how much more do we need to devote ourselves to prayer to our God as we build our domestic church?

If you are seeking some guidance in prayer, a popular structure that may be helpful is called the ACTS prayer. ACTS is an acronym for Adoration, Contrition, Thanksgiving, and Supplication, four types of prayer that can lead us to a well-rounded prayer life. Let's examine each of these types of prayers.

Adoration: In adoration, we focus on our love for God. Jesus told us that we are to love God with all our heart, being, mind, and strength (Luke 10:27), and adoration helps us focus on doing just that. Additionally in adoration, we pause to acknowledge whom we are praying to: the Creator of the universe, who despite his glory and awesome power, invites us to call him Father and has numbered all the hairs on our head (Luke 12:7). Contemplating this may give us the proper attitude in prayer.

"Shout joyfully to the LORD, all you lands; serve the LORD with gladness; come before him with joyful song. Know that the LORD is God, he made us, we belong to him, we are his people, the flock he shepherds" (Psalm 100:1–3).

Contrition/Confession: If we love someone, we seek that person's forgiveness when we offend him or her. In contrition, we ask God's forgiveness for our sins. We should reflect for a short while and try to be specific in contrition. This will help us to be more loving and obedient children tomorrow. From Scripture we may pray the simple prayer of the tax collector, "O God, be merciful to me a sinner" (Luke 18:13). Jesus praised this prayer, saying that all who exalt themselves will be humbled, and the one who humbles himself will be exalted. If you and your spouse are praying together, this is the perfect time to ask each other's forgiveness as well.

Thanksgiving: We have found that being parents has given us a new perspective on our relationship with our heavenly Father. The boundless love we have for our children gives us just a glimpse of the magnitude of God's love for us, his children. And when the objects of our love pause in their play to say, "Thank you, mom! Thank you, dad!" it does our hearts good, just as God must be pleased when we give thanks for our many blessings. The Blessed Mother prayed, "The Mighty One has done great things for me, and holy is his name" (Luke 1:49). We also have much to be grateful for as we grow into a family.

Supplication: This prayer may be the most natural to us as we stand on the verge of parenthood, because in supplication, we ask for God's help. Oftentimes we may view this prayer as somehow less than the others, but it really isn't. It shows our reliance, our dependence, and our faith in our God. Even in the Our Father, we ask for daily sustenance: "Give us this day our daily bread" (Matthew 6:11). Scripture is full of the faithful's calling on God's assistance, and a simple, heartfelt prayer of supplication comes from King David: "Graciously rescue me, God! Come quickly to help me, LORD!" (Psalm 70:2).

Questions for him

If you were to pray only a prayer of supplication today, for what would you ask God for special help? What specifically about your wife are you thankful for?

Share with your wife a prayer of thanksgiving for her.

Questions for her

One of the most famous lines in Scripture spoken by the Blessed Mother is, "Behold, I am the handmaid of the Lord. May it be done to me according to your word" (Luke 1:38). How might Mary's words inspire you in your prayer life? How might this attitude of faith empower you in your role of mother? What specifically about your husband are you thankful for?

Share with your husband a prayer of thanksgiving for him.

Questions for both

If you don't yet pray together, what are your thoughts on starting this practice? If you do, share your feelings about this practice with your spouse. Would you like to use the ACTS format together? Why or why not?

Prayer

Dear heavenly Father, we love you as our creator and the author of all life. Please forgive us for every offense against you and against each other. We are endlessly grateful that we have been called to become mother and father to one of your precious children. Please guide us in wisdom as we prepare to build our domestic church, and keep our hearts full of wonder at your creation and the gift of life. We pray this in the name of the Father, and of the Son, and of the Holy Spirit. Amen.

2. Defying the Odds

Love is patient, love is kind.
It is not jealous, [love] is not pompous,
it is not inflated, it is not rude,
it does not seek its own interests,
it is not quick-tempered,
it does not brood over injury,
it does not rejoice over wrongdoing
but rejoices with the truth.
It bears all things, believes all things,
hopes all things, endures all things.
Love never fails.

1 CORINTHIANS 13:4–8

As we mentioned in the Introduction, research indicates a drop in marital satisfaction for many couples during the child-rearing years. However, the great news is that about 35 percent of couples do not experience this decline, and some actually experience an increase in satisfaction and intimacy. Researchers have examined the factors that increase our odds of being in this happy group. Their findings are simple and encouraging, and they suggest that we can cultivate a few habits that could make a real difference in our marriage as we transition into parenthood.

Three chapters in this book are devoted to the buffers that help prevent disharmony: marital spirituality/prayer, the sexual relationship, and division of household chores. These issues topped the list of factors that greatly affected a couple's marital satisfaction. (See chapters 1, 3, and 8.) The remaining factors are discussed in this section.

- *Having a true awareness of our spouse's world.* This means having an understanding of what our partner is going through, what stresses he or she is experiencing, what demands he or she may be dealing with at work, and anything else that affects his or her life outside of the marriage. The idea is basically to remind ourselves that our spouse has needs, anxieties, fears, and stressors as real as ours. It may seem puzzling at first that this would make such a difference in a marriage, but let's consider how this focus on attentiveness and awareness can help us as we become parents. Compare the following:

Low Awareness	High Awareness
"You sure are grumpy today."	"I bet you're exhausted after being up so much with the baby last night."
"I can't stand how tense you act nowadays."	"I know Wednesdays are especially busy and stressful at your office. Let's try to relax together for a few minutes."
"Why don't you ever listen to me?"	"I know it's hard to focus when the baby is cranky. Can we talk later?"

We can begin to imagine how the low-awareness comments can start a huge fight, while the high-awareness comments can lead to great appreciation and understanding. As new parents, our focus will tend to be on the new baby's needs, and then on our own. It's easy to forget that our spouse is experiencing his or her own struggles as well. A little acknowledgment of this can go a long way toward marital harmony.

- *Expressing admiration and fondness for our spouse.* At first glance this may just seem like a nice habit that may make life a little more pleasant. However, when we feel insecure as new parents, this habit can make all the difference in how we feel about ourselves and our spouse.

Situation	Expression of Admiration
Mom is struggling with an inconsolable infant and begins to feel she is a failure because she thinks she should be able to effectively comfort her own baby.	Dad sees her anxiety and says, "You are so patient with him. I knew you'd be a great mom."
Dad worries that the baby is not really bonding with him and says, "I don't think he even likes me."	Mom says, "I admire how gentle you are with him. He can feel how much you love him."
Mom is stressed because the house no longer looks as tidy as she would like. "I can't keep up!" she cries.	"We're doing fine," dad soothes. "I don't know how you accomplish all that you do in a day with a new baby. Tell me how I can help."

In all three situations, a few kind words help mom and dad go from feeling like failures to feeling like winners, or at least to feeling loved and understood.

- *Generosity.* Spouses who viewed their partner as generous reported higher levels of satisfaction than others. This generosity was not exhibited by gift giving, but by simple acts of service, regular displays of affection, and a willingness to forgive each other. In fact, researchers found that happy couples averaged five positive comments and interactions for each negative interaction. Generosity takes on new significance when we feel especially stressed, as we do when caring for a new baby.

Situation	Generosity Displayed
Dad was up half the night with the baby. When he gets out of bed in the morning, he finds his wife has his coffee ready and waiting.	Act of service
New mom has had no time or energy to get made up or dressed up for days and complains of feeling unattractive. New dad gives her a long hug and says, "You're more beautiful than ever."	Display of affection

Situation	Generosity Displayed
Sleep-deprived dad is more irritable and short-tempered than usual. After snapping at mom for the third time, he says, "I'm sorry. I'm just so tired." Rather than becoming indignant, she responds, "I understand. Try to get some rest this afternoon."	Forgiveness

In each of these scenarios, we see each spouse generously coming to the other's emotional "rescue," helping each other to feel loved in stressful moments.

- **Commitment**. Marital satisfaction remained higher for spouses who expressed a serious intent to remain together through good times and bad and maintained the belief that they had found the best mate for themselves. If we think of this in terms of baby-raising, we may begin to glimpse the significance of this factor. When caring for an infant twenty-four hours a day, both husband and wife are more dependent on each other than when they were childless. Prior to baby, both may have been highly successful, independent, confident individuals, needing little more from each other than affection and companionship. Sure, they were committed, but in a relaxed "we enjoy life together" kind of way. After the baby, each is literally dependent on the other. Perhaps the husband returns to work a few days after the birth while the wife stays home. After caring for a new baby for ten hours, the new mother needs, in a very real way, her husband's help as soon as he returns home. She is unaccustomed to feeling needy and dependent and must sense that her husband is 100 percent committed to the family for her to openly share this need. She must sense that her "I need you" will be met with his "I am committed to you." Likewise, dad may feel that nothing he does with baby is good enough (a fairly common complaint). If mom focuses on criticizing his efforts, she is not communicating a sense of commitment; rather, she is communicating that he may not be as good as other fathers and husbands.

Situation	Commitment Response	Noncommitment Response
Mom is feeling the effects of dealing with a colicky baby all day. Dad called to say he would be working late. Her silence tells him something is wrong.	"Is everything OK? What can I do for you?"	"Listen, it's no picnic here at work, either!"

Situation	Commitment Response	Noncommitment Response
Dad has bought yet another toy that is too advanced for the new baby. Mom realizes that he feels she criticizes his parenting a lot.	"What a sweet daddy! Always thinking of his boy."	"How many times have I told you..."

The commitment response simply communicates that we love and accept our spouse and have a genuine desire to meet his or her needs, while the noncommitment response communicates that the spouse is flawed, imperfect, and not quite good enough.

Research suggests that for simple changes in behavior to become habit, they must be practiced for about sixty days. As you study the lists in this section, what habits should you consider cultivating between now and baby's arrival?

Questions for him

How comfortable are you in openly expressing your admiration and love for your wife? What would you like to share with her now?

Decide which of the factors in this section you might struggle with the most. Ask Saint Joseph, patron saint of fathers, to pray for you.

Question for her

New fathers can sometimes feel they are not as capable in caregiving as their wives are. What traits does your husband possess that will make him a strong and capable father? Express your admiration for these traits.

Decide which of the factors in this section you might struggle with the most. Ask the Blessed Mother to pray for you.

Questions for both

Research recommends that we be generous in our acts of service, expressions of affection and forgiveness. Which of these makes you feel most loved? What stressors outside of your marriage does your spouse experience? How can you show you care about these?

Prayer

Dear Lord, we thank you for this sacrament of marriage that we hold so dear. We know that strengthening our marriage is pleasing to you, pleasing to us, and beneficial for our children. We ask for your guidance as we transition into this new chapter of our marriage. As our family grows, we ask that you teach us to grow in generosity, compassion, and intimacy. Amen.

3. Your Sexual Relationship

I belong to my lover,
and my lover belongs to me.

Song of Songs 6:3

As you approach parenthood, you have probably given some thought as to how your sexual relationship will be affected by that little bundle of joy. You may wonder if all the jokes and stories about this aspect of parenting could possibly be true.

Sex is indeed on hold in the first weeks and then less frequent in the first months after childbirth. Although this is not encouraging news, don't despair. With a little patience and attention, you can soon return to enjoying a satisfying sexual relationship. Some couples find they discover new sides of each other when they become parents, which adds excitement to their relationship and love life. But since the majority of couples do hit a few snags along the way, let's examine some of the underlying issues commonly encountered.

- Physically, a woman needs time to heal after childbirth. Sexual intercourse will be off-limits for a time. Even after healing, a woman often feels insecure about perceived changes to her body resulting from childbirth. This leaves her feeling less desirable and sexual. (Adoptive moms, you won't deal with this issue, but you will deal with all the rest.)

- Both partners will be busier and more fatigued, leaving less energy for sex. As much as you enjoy being intimate with each other, sleep needs usually trump sexual desires. Added stress and anxiety don't put anybody in "the mood," and early on, you're dealing with plenty of both.

- Husbands and wives may have mismatched levels of desire for a while. Hormonal fluctuations may affect new mom's libido for a time. Additionally, babies are usually quite literally attached to their mothers. All that physical closeness can sometimes lead a wife to desire a little "hands-off" time.

What's a loving spouse to do? Accept a platonic relationship in place of an affectionate, sexual one? No! Each of the hurdles just mentioned can be dealt with.

- Wives, you will be happy to know that husbands do not experience less pleasure in lovemaking after baby. You may feel childbirth has caused dramatic physical changes, but your husband will not agree. Some aspects of sex may change for you for a while, though. For instance, some women experience pain early on during intercourse. Be open about this with your husband so that he can be especially attentive to your needs and make necessary adjustments. Beyond physical changes, a woman may need additional encouragement and compliments from her husband to feel amorous since her body may not look like she'd like it to right away. Husbands, it may be helpful to encourage your wife to take some time to making herself feel attractive. This may include a manicure, a haircut, or a new outfit. Generally, the more attractive she feels, the more romantic she feels.

- To combat busyness, fatigue, and anxiety, you may have to change things up a bit. You might find, for instance, that you have more energy for lovemaking early in the day rather than at night. Many couples find it helpful to let go of the notion that sex must be spontaneous. Daily life is more scheduled than ever with a baby, so why not schedule some pleasurable time too? It will give both of you something to look forward to. A note on busyness: Wives who felt that household chores were fairly divided were more likely to feel that their marriage was sexually satisfying. Reading between the lines, we might conclude that these wives were less fatigued and frustrated and so had more energy and desire for sex.

- It's perfectly normal for one spouse to feel more amorous than the other, depending on the day and circumstances. Generally, whoever feels more tired and stressed will feel less sexual. As is usually the case, communication is the key. Gently explaining to your spouse that you are really exhausted, distracted, or tense can begin a constructive conversation. The two of you might come up with suggestions to get you back to feeling normal. Without clearly communicating the problem, an iciness may develop. One will feel rejected, the other mis-understood. Resentment will begin to build, killing any chance of romance.

A decrease in sexual activity, however, should not mean a decrease in physical affection. In fact, it may be more important than ever. A snuggle, a back rub, or a warm hug and kiss can help keep tender feelings alive. Too many couples fear that any sort of physical gesture may signal sex they are not ready for. Be open about this with each other, and express your need and enjoyment of nonsexual physical affection.

As you find yourselves navigating this temporary adjustment period, try to maintain a relaxed attitude. Adding pressure or unreasonable expectations, keeping score, and comparing yourselves to others or to your life before baby will do nothing to increase intimacy. Try instead to aim for an extra dose of understanding and affection, open communication, and patience. You'll both reap the benefits, not only in the sexual realm, but in your whole marital relationship.

Questions for him

If your wife's sexual desire decreases for a while after childbirth, how might you feel? How do you currently help your wife feel attractive?

Questions for her

Are you at all concerned about changes to your body after childbirth? If so, share your concerns with your husband. What helps you to feel attractive? What do you imagine may help you to feel attractive later when you are a new mom?

Question for both

What are your thoughts or feelings as you reflect on the opening Scripture verse?

Prayer

Dear Lord, you said that husband and wife shall become "one flesh" (Matthew 19:5), underscoring how intimate and close their relationship should be. Please give us the patience, love, and understanding to nurture our sexual relationship through every phase of our marriage.

4. Time for Each Other

Love one another with mutual affection;
anticipate one another in showing honor.

Imagine the following scenario: You come home from a tough day at work. Your spouse senses something is wrong and offers to give you a relaxing back rub and lend an understanding ear. Later, over a quiet dinner and a glass of wine, you feel a sense of peace and appreciation for this understanding partner.

Fast-forward some months and imagine this scenario: You have the worst day at work. When you arrive home, your spouse looks more harried than ever. The baby is exhausted and fussy but refused to nap all day. You realize, correctly, that this is not the time to seek sympathy for the bad day at the office; it's time to lend a hand.

Contrasting these scenarios drives home the point that when your baby arrives, he or she becomes the focus of your emotional energy. This is normal and necessary. We submerge our own needs to provide appropriate care for those dependent on us. However, it is important to realize that we need not and should not neglect each other's emotional needs indefinitely. Although we will no longer be immediately tending to every whim, thought, and concern as we used to, it's vital that we regularly take time to reconnect with our spouse.

Upon hearing this advice, new parents often shrug it off as unrealistic. "Who has time?" they ask. Babies require constant attention, and the list of baby-related chores can seem endless. Since time is at a premium, here are some potential daily opportunities for maintaining emotional closeness.

- **Driving**. Babies often nod off or become mesmerized on the road, giving you some precious quiet time together. Turn off the radio, silence the cell phone, and take some time to listen to each other.

- **Lying down together**. Although it's tempting to stay up late to catch up on a favorite television show while your spouse goes to bed, try to take a few quiet minutes to lie down together to reconnect.

- **Housework**. As we will discuss in chapter 8, household chores multiply once baby arrives, and baby's naptime is the prime opportunity for tending to them. If possible, occasionally work in the same area of the house so you can chat while working. Don't forget that you need not be busy every second baby is asleep. Sitting down for a cup of coffee together can be time well spent.

- **Exercise**. Many new moms are focused on getting back their pre-baby bodies, and strolling with the new baby is great exercise. Dads, why not join mom for fresh air, exercise, and conversation?

- **E-connecting**. Whether you're both at work or one of you stays home with baby, use your e-mail or texting to keep in touch. A simple "thinking of you" or "miss you" can warm your beloved's heart. Sending an interesting article or bit of news can provide a conversation-starter for later. Short phone calls are great too, but if one partner is particularly busy, a text message may be better received.

If the previous suggestions are snacks that can keep your relationship from starving, date night (or morning or afternoon) is Thanksgiving dinner—indulgent, leisurely, and satisfying. Happily married parents swear by regular date nights that add romance and revitalize the relationship. Some OB-GYNs believe so strongly in the power of the date that they require new moms to have had an honest-to-goodness date by their six-week postpartum checkup.

Speaking from experience, we can say that nothing beats the feeling of total relaxation that comes from leaving your baby or toddler in trustworthy, capable hands and sitting down to a quiet meal together. As a new parent, those early weeks and months can have you in constant "on" mode, feeling like you must be ready to spring into action at any second. It is refreshing and restorative to flip our internal switch to off for just a couple of hours.

If a little voice in your head is telling you that you can't afford a sitter and a meal out, don't despair. We have found that the best babysitting scenario for our peace of mind and pocketbook is forming a babysitting co-op with a trusted family with children of a similar age. Each of us couples gets a regular date with no babysitting fees. As an added bonus, our children are so happy to see one another that we have no guilt about leaving them. Grandparents and aunts and uncles may be delighted to keep baby for a few hours as well. As for the date itself, inexpensive restaurants work just as well as expensive ones, and there is something charming and romantic about a simple picnic in the park.

We've all heard the old adage that little things mean a lot, and when it comes to keeping our relationships close and warm, they truly do. Grand vacations and five-star restaurants are lovely and enjoyable but probably unrealistic at this time. If we wait for the opportunity to share such spectacular events, we'll miss out on numerous other chances to reconnect. As we venture into parenthood, we probably need text messages more than sky writing, a shared burger more than a $100 steak, and a short hike around the neighborhood more than a stroll on an exotic beach.

Question for him

What did you think or feel as you read the two contrasting scenarios at the beginning of this chapter?

Share with your wife your ideal post-baby date.

Questions for her

Which of the daily opportunities for closeness do you think might work best for you? Can you add to the list?

Share with your husband fond memories of your recent dates.

Questions for both

What outings do you and your husband currently enjoy together? How might these be affected by the arrival of baby? Who might you most trust as a babysitter? How often at this point would you ideally like to get away for a date?

Prayer

Dear Lord, you have blessed us with a loving marriage. We ask for your guidance, that we may be ever mindful of how to nurture our marital vocation as we embark on our vocation of parenthood.

5. Time for Self

You formed my inmost being;
you knit me in my mother's womb.
I praise you, because I am wonderfully made;
wonderful are your works!

PSALM 139:13–14

Did you do a double-take when you read this section's title? First, you're becoming increasingly aware of how time-consuming a baby will be. Then we discussed the importance of taking time each day to nurture your marriage. Now you're supposed to carve out time for yourself? Well, yes.

Although it might be unrealistic to expect to devote as much time to hobbies and socializing as you did pre-baby, taking time to pursue your passions, periods of solitude, and time with friends is vital to your emotional and spiritual health. And when you're fulfilled, you're a better spouse and parent.

In this section we want to emphasize the importance of giving yourself and your spouse permission to take time out for self. Consider the following activities and how rejuvenating they could be to you, your spouse, and your family.

- Time praying before the Blessed Sacrament
- An hour in a bookstore, browsing or reading
- Meeting a close friend for lunch or coffee
- A solitary walk in nature
- A couple of hours spent doing something purely for enjoyment—whether it be shopping, knitting, painting, woodworking, and so forth

- Taking part in a Bible study or other faith-formation group
- Getting together with friends for the big game

As we review the list, we can see that each activity, in its own way, gets at who we really are. For instance, at your core you could be a nature lover who savors a good hike. You probably don't want to entirely neglect this aspect of yourself, nor should you. Try to preserve those activities most meaningful to you, but realize that you will probably need to scale back somewhat.

When you fell in love with your spouse, you were probably intrigued by his or her interests and passions. After all, that's what made this person distinct from everybody else you knew. As parenting begins, it will be less convenient for each of you to carve out alone time, so try to encourage your partner to do just that. Oftentimes, it is helpful to encourage your spouse to get away from the house for some alone time. However, it is also a good idea to let your beloved have the house to him/herself on occasion without a to-do list. Everyone could benefit from a little quiet time in a usually busy home. Many parents will be so preoccupied with meeting their baby's and spouse's needs that they will never request time alone or away, even though they could use it. For this reason, you may find it best to schedule regular periods of "alone time" hours so that they need not be requested.

Question for him

What hobbies, spiritual practices, or social outlets does your wife treasure most?

Question for her

What hobbies, spiritual practices, or social outlets does your husband treasure most?

Question for both

How do you feel when you take time to pursue a favorite activity? Share those feelings with your spouse.

Prayer

Dear Lord, as Scripture says, we are "wonderfully made" (Psalm 139:14). Thank you for creating us with our own unique personalities, talents, and interests. When we become parents, we will be focused on fulfilling the duties of our new roles. Please help us generously encourage each other to preserve and nurture our innermost selves.

6. Friendship

If the one falls, the other will help the fallen one.
But woe to the solitary person!
If that one should fall,
there is no other to help.

ECCLESIASTES 4:10

Many of the topics we discuss in this book may already be familiar to you. For instance, we often hear parents joke about sleep or sex issues, and sometimes a friend will talk about the importance of date nights or complain about household chores. However, the topic of changes in friendship is talked about less often, even though it is a common phenomenon.

Consider some of the activities you currently enjoy with your friends: movies, shopping excursions, dinner, maybe even weekend trips. These are enjoyable times, and no doubt your friends are great, fun people. If they are not yet parents, however, there is a chance your friendship will be somewhat altered after you go from childless buddies to conscientious parents. The activities you have typically shared won't necessarily fit your new lifestyle.

As is key to so many changes, this one is easier to accept if you can anticipate and prepare for it. Here are some points to consider.

- Not all friendships will necessarily be altered when your baby arrives. Some of your pals will remain as close as ever. However, you may have some friends who have no interest in children and may only enjoy adult activities, like expensive dinners out, meeting for drinks, movies, or vacationing. This is OK—it's who they are.

If you should find that they are habitually absent for a good while as you parent, try not to take offense. Meeting at the park and pushing Junior in the swing may be of little interest to them. It's hard not to be hurt if someone you love is disinterested in your child, but we often have to accept what we cannot change. These friends would probably enjoy a get-together without your little one, and when possible, try to arrange such an outing.

- It is also very possible that your childless friends do not understand the demands of parenthood and may be a bit miffed that you are not as available as you once were. Or they may view you as a little (or a lot!) obsessed with your baby, a sign that the two of you now have little in common. Try to be understanding and carve out time for your friends as is feasible, but don't stress too much. You only have so many hours in a day, and you are perfectly normal if you are obsessed with that new bundle of love and a little overwhelmed with day-to-day responsibilities. A big part of friendship is empathy, and it needs to be exhibited on both sides.

- It may be helpful to accept that your friendships will go through various changes and phases. If you accept this concept, you will be less likely to feel hurt or fret that your friendships are over. Maybe you can't do your weekly night out, but in this new phase of your friendship, perhaps you can keep up with phone calls, e-mail, and occasional morning coffees. Think about friends you had in school or at a job. Once you no longer had school or job in common, your relationship probably changed somewhat. But if they were real friends, you probably still keep in touch.

- It may have been a while since you've had to make new friends. Some folks who live in their original hometown may have had the same friends since grade school. Others settled comfortably into the social scene at work years ago. However, in this new phase of adulthood, many of us form new and rewarding friendships with fellow new parents. It's hard to describe how comforting and helpful it is to have good, trustworthy friends meeting the same joys and challenges of this phase of life. The benefits are endless. These friends are willing to share tips that work for them for teething, sleep issues, potty training, and everything between. They empathize with your crisis of the day, and they understand your "obsession" because they are equally obsessed. Their homes are perfectly kid-friendly places where your child is always a welcome playmate. They focus on child-friendly get-togethers and outings but understand the need for couple date nights and will be your most trusted babysitters. They also understand girls'/guys' nights out but realize these need to be scheduled around children's dinnertime, bath time, breastfeeding, and so forth. In short, they are priceless!

How do we go about finding such friends? The following organizations are good starters: childbirth or breastfeeding classes, adoption groups, church nurseries, and area moms'/parents' groups. The key in all venues is to keep your eyes open for folks you click with, and by all means don't be afraid to extend the first invitation for a get-together. You and your new friends will be so glad you did. All the parents in our neighborhood are forever grateful to the mom who put a notice in the neighborhood newsletter inviting families to a play date in the park. It turned out that a huge number of families were looking for friendship and support, and the club is more active than ever. Through this group, we have met our dearest new parent friends.

Questions for him

What activities do you and your friends enjoy together? How might these need to be adjusted once your child arrives?

Question for her

What qualities do you look for in a friend?

Questions for both

How comfortable are you approaching potential friends? Do you know any parents or parents-to-be?

Prayer

Lord, we are so grateful for the friends you have given us. They are but one of the many joys and blessings in our lives. We pray that we may be able to maintain these friendships as they evolve in the coming years. As our roles change, please help us to befriend other new parents with whom to share our joys and struggles.

7. Parenting Differences

A mild answer turns back wrath,
but a harsh word stirs up anger.

PROVERBS 15:1

No matter how happy, no matter how loving, every couple has disagreements. When you first set up a household together, you may have disagreed about where the couch should be or what color to paint the hallway. In the end, you compromised or one of you just gave in, and in the end it didn't really matter that much to either of you.

Fast-forward to the parenting years. There are hundreds of decisions to be made, but this time the decisions concern your number-one priority, your bundle of joy, your sweet little angel, your darling child. You may have differing ideas on a host of baby issues, such as co-sleeping, rocking to sleep, pacifier, television, naps, expensive organic foods and products, and later a host of child issues, such as private or public school, spanking, time-outs, chores.

Compromise? Give in? Not this time. This is a whole new level of disagreement. Emotions can run high and tempers can flare. What to do?

- Realize that neither of you has all the right answers, and each of you loves your child. Each of you has an opinion and wants to do what is best. Sometimes one or both partners become convinced that their way is the only way. For example, Kate felt she was the only one capable of putting her son to bed. However, when she was suffering with a nasty flu bug, she had to relinquish control and allow husband, Keith, to put her dear boy to bed. It turned out that baby didn't actually need the long and wearisome process Kate had invented. In this case, mom was quite delighted to discover that dad had some good, though differing, ideas.

- When you are at odds on an issue, a little objective research can help. When Stacy and Cliff struggled to get their eleven-month-old to sleep through the night, Stacy remembered hearing that some babies need to "cry it out" for a few nights. Cliff was horrified and thought Stacy was cruel to even suggest it. A little research revealed that many parents swear by the strategy, while other parents and experts are staunchly opposed to the practice. Cliff was less horrified knowing that many good, caring parents used the method, and Stacy was more understanding of Cliff's hesitation. In the end, they decided to try a modified "cry it out" approach with which they were both reasonably comfortable.

- When parenting, we can get very anxious about a great many issues—some of them more important than others. Before we get too worked up and dig in our heels on an issue, we may want to stop and ask, "Is this something that will really affect my child's well-being and development or am I possibly blowing this out of proportion?" If baby gets off the bottle at thirteen months rather than at twelve months, is he really doomed to dental ruin? If one parent wants to let him watch a baby DVD when both had originally planned on a "no TV" rule, is he really headed for cognitive impairment? Most of the time we could stand to remind ourselves to relax and not let a minor issue turn into a point of contention. If you're not sure if this is an ISSUE or an issue, a little research and discussion with some experienced parents might help you decide.

As you navigate various disagreements related to parenting, try to keep in mind the opening Scripture verse from Proverbs. When both partners feel strongly about an issue, ask God to help you both remain mild-mannered and avoid harsh words.

Question for him

Some fathers feel they must defer to mothers on parenting issues. Do you think you have this mindset at this point? Share your thoughts with your wife.

Question for her

What resources (friends, family, books) are informing your views on various parenting issues? Share what you have been learning and thinking about with your husband.

Questions for both

How have you resolved differences of opinion on important issues in the past? Is there room for improvement in your handling of these differences? Share your feelings. Can you foresee any issues about which you may differ? Begin a constructive dialogue.

Prayer

Dear Lord, we feel a great sense of responsibility in our new vocation as parents. Along with that sense of responsibility come anxiety and the potential for conflict. We pray for your wisdom and gentle spirit to guide us to make good decisions and keep a peaceful home.

8. Household and Baby Chores

Have the same regard for one another.

ROMANS 12:16

As a married couple, you likely know that the division of household labor is no small issue. Resentment can quickly build if one partner feels the other is not doing his or her fair share. Interestingly, both partners are usually convinced that they are the ones doing the most work. "I did all the vacuuming and laundry while he sat there watching the game," fumes the wife. "I cleaned the bathrooms and the gutters while she went out with her girlfriends," mopes the husband. Neither one sees what the other did, as each is so focused on his or her own accomplishments. Feelings on this topic run so high that research has found that among nonmarried, cohabiting couples, household chores are a prime reason for breakups.

Now enters the baby. Your list of things to do just grew exponentially. Who is going to empty the diaper pail, bathe the baby, clip her fingernails and toenails, put her to bed, get up in the night with her, feed her breakfast? Other household chores grow in volume as well. For instance, there is more laundry (yes, those little outfits add up!), more grocery shopping (diapers, formula, baby food, wipes), more dishes, and more tidying up due to the abundance of toys and supplies.

Rather than venturing down the treacherous road of "I Do More Than You," we suggest you take expert advice and divide up every chore you can think of, baby and nonbaby related. Below is a list of baby-related chores to get you started. For many of these, you will likely answer, "Both of us," but be specific. If, for instance, you are both going to be changing diapers, try to decide on a time of day for each, say morning and afternoon for mom and evenings for dad. Otherwise somewhere along the line, one of you will become Diaper Parent without realizing it and may get resentful that the other has sidestepped this rather thankless task.

- Feeding
- Diaper changes
- Dressing
- Clipping nails
- Bathing
- Cleaning the tub, putting away bath toys
- Naptime routine
- Disinfecting baby's toys
- Tidying various rooms
- Putting away baby's clothes
- Emptying diaper pail
- Comforting baby during nighttime wake-ups
- Taking baby to/from daycare
- Packing the diaper bag
- Organizing baby supplies (diapers, wipes, lotions)

Additionally, baby demands almost constant supervision/stimulation/interaction. This is the most fun, delightful, and heartwarming part of parenting. However, if one parent is the daytime caregiver, as lovely as baby-parent interaction is, he or she will appreciate a little break from it, and baby will enjoy focused attention from the other parent. Consider planning on an agreed-upon amount of evening time for this.

With a little forethought and planning, your household can run smoothly, with each partner knowing his or her roles and responsibilities. The key is not to critique the job your spouse is doing.

Question for him

How well do you think your household runs now? Discuss.

Question for her

How fairly are household chores currently divided? Discuss.

Question for both

How did you feel as you divided up baby chores?

Prayer

Dear Lord, as we prepare to become parents, we realize we will both be busier than ever. Please help us to be peaceful and efficient as we tend to all the tasks of our household. We pray that we may always be grateful that we have a home to clean, food to buy and prepare, and most of all, a dear child to love and care for.

9. Get Out!

This is the day the LORD has made;
let us rejoice in it and be glad.

PSALM 118:24

In this pre-baby life, it's likely the two of you are out and about quite a bit. Restaurants, movies, sporting events, and parties are probably common outings. When the baby arrives, it's not uncommon to spend much more time within the home. Some parents grow weary of spending so much time confined, and if this feeling festers for too long, irritability and restlessness may build. Irritable spouses bicker, and things can go downhill from there. Fortunately, being sequestered is not a prerequisite of good parenting, and much of our exile is needlessly self-imposed. While pediatricians recommend avoiding crowds (germy!) for the first two months of life since little one has not received any vaccines yet, getting out even in those early weeks is feasible and advisable.

Early on, we may find it difficult to even think of what might be an appropriate outing for an infant. We hope the following list may spark some ideas:

- Find out when your church doors are open and stop by to pray. The holy silence and beauty of the church is restorative to the soul. Better yet, find out when adoration is available and schedule your visit accordingly.

- If the weather is nice, a brisk walk in fresh air is invigorating. If it's just too frigid, try a morning walk at a shopping mall. (Holding baby in a carrier on your back or front will keep germy strangers' hands at bay.)

- Even if baby is too young to play, a trip to the nearest park is a good change of scenery (and a possible opportunity to meet new parents). Ditto for the zoo and museums, which are likely to be more engaging to parents than to infants early on, which is fine.

- Arrange to visit a (nonsick!) friend or family member. Very often, they will feel they should come to visit the new family, but explain that you need a little outing, and they will probably be happy to host.

- As baby gets a little older, some companies specialize in play "classes" for parent and child, and public libraries usually offer story hours. These are not just a pleasant experience for both baby and parent but a chance to meet more parents.

- Plan a "play date" with a well baby, even if your baby spends the date sleeping in his carrier. Chatting with fellow new parents is good for your mental health.

- Get outside for a simple, little-to-no-planning-required picnic. It can be in the backyard, a park, or a nature preserve.

- Take a car ride in the country or to an out-of-the way destination. Babies can be mesmerized and relaxed by a trip in the car, and we all have those places we keep meaning to visit.

A wise pediatrician once advised a group of parents-to-be that we tend to be concerned about doing what is best for the baby, and we need to realize that we should also think in terms of what is best for the family. If the family needs an outing, don't fret that baby may nap in the car rather than in his comfy crib. He'll be fine and will benefit from having reinvigorated, energized parents.

Question for him

Do you feel restless or restored when you stay at home? Explain.

Questions for her

Have you thought about how your ability to get out for fun may be curtailed? What are your feelings?

Questions for both

Which of the baby-friendly outings on the list appeal to you? Can you add two more that are appropriate to your specific situation?

Prayer

Dear Lord, we savor the active life we enjoy as a couple. Please help us to be mindful of healthy ways to get out and enjoy your beautiful world with our new bundle of joy.

10. Postpartum Depression

Do not fear: I am with you;
do not be anxious: I am your God.
I will strengthen you, I will help you,
I will uphold you with my
victorious right hand.

ISAIAH 41:10

If you're feeling overwhelmed and a little blue following the arrival of baby, remember that these are normal reactions. Once things settle down, hormones begin to return to normal, and a routine begins to emerge. You should start feeling like your old self again.

But what if you don't? It's important to recognize that about 10 to 15 percent of mothers and 10 percent of fathers develop postpartum depression, a major form of depression that should be treated as soon as possible. Symptoms include sadness, crying, loss of interest in life (maybe even loss of interest in the baby), fatigue, trouble concentrating, and problems with appetite and sleeping. Unlike the very common "baby blues," these symptoms persist rather than decrease in the weeks following birth.

As we discuss in chapter 12 on your emotional reaction to baby, the key is to acknowledge your feelings and those of your partner. Too often, parents feel guilty for experiencing depressive symptoms and therefore do not seek support from their spouse or treatment from their physician. If left untreated, postpartum depression not only affects the parents' mental health but also negatively impacts a baby's development. So keep honest communication going with your spouse, accept each other's feelings as legitimate, and encourage each other to seek help if you suspect depression.

To help reduce your chances of developing symptoms in the first place, experts offer a couple of simple recommendations. First, have a support network in place before baby arrives. Being isolated is a risk factor for developing postpartum depression, as it adds to our feelings of being overwhelmed, stressed out, and sad. As our friend Mary described, "I felt like I didn't have a friend in the world." Mary had quit her job to stay home with her son and soon discovered that all of her friends were coworkers, her family lived too far away to visit much, and her days were long and lonely. She endured some difficult months before finding neighborhood moms with little ones. She quickly realized that having supportive friends to turn to helped her manage her new responsibilities and increased her sense of well-being. Review the section on friendship if you feel your support network is not what it needs to be.

Excessive fatigue is another predictor of postpartum depression. We've devoted a whole section (13) to the importance of sleep, but it's worth repeating here: Take all reasonable measures to maximize your hours of sleep each day. A tired parent can quickly become a depressed parent! Look to each other, to your support network, and to hired babysitters for help if sleep deprivation is affecting your mood.

To combat depression spiritually, you may spend some time together with Scripture, reflecting on verses focused on God's unending care and compassion, like the one introducing this section. These additional ones may also be helpful:

> "The LORD is good to those who wait for him, a refuge on the day of distress, taking care of those who look to him for protection, when the flood rages" (Nahum 1:7–8).

> "I command you: be strong and steadfast! Do not fear nor be dismayed, for the LORD, your God, is with you wherever you go" (Joshua 1:9).

> "The Lord is a stronghold for the oppressed, a stronghold in times of trouble" (Psalm 9:10).

> "When cares increase within me, your comfort gives me joy" (Psalm 94:19).

> "Have no anxiety at all, but in everything, by prayer and petition, with thanksgiving, make your requests known to God. Then the peace of God that surpasses all understanding will guard your hearts and minds in Christ Jesus" (Philippians 4:6–7).

> "I have the strength for everything through him who empowers me" (Philippians 4:13).

> "Cast all your worries upon him because he cares for you" (1 Peter 5:7).

John 11 includes Jesus' compassion to Mary and Martha who lost their brother. This story can remind us that Jesus walks with us throughout our trials.

In the Gospel of Luke, Jesus cures the hemorrhaging woman who dared to touch him, telling her, "Daughter, your faith has saved you; go in peace" (8:48) This teaches us that we are to reach out to Jesus when we suffer.

Question for him

Are you already experiencing a variety of emotions regarding the upcoming arrival of your child? If so, share these with your wife.

Questions for her

How close is your relationship with your physician? Can you openly share any concerns with him/her?

Questions for both

What Bible verse speaks most to your heart? Why? Can you think of a time when you, like the hemorrhaging woman, reached out to God in faith and desperation during a difficult time?

Prayer

Dear Lord, as we look forward to the arrival of our child, we imagine that we will feel joy, excitement, and gratitude even during the challenging times, though we realize we may struggle more than we would like. We ask for your light to guide us through our darkest hours that we may, with your help, be able to feel the joy the psalmist felt when he wrote, "This is the day the LORD has made; let us rejoice in it and be glad" (Psalm 118:24).

11. Grandparents

Listen to your father who begot you,
do not despise your mother when she is old.

PROVERBS 23:22

"You tell her to leave, or I will," our friend Veronica commanded her husband a few days postpartum. She was referring, unfortunately, to her mother-in-law, who had traveled some distance to spend a few days with the new baby. We still wince when we think about the position Veronica's husband was in.

What on earth could lead a new mom to giving Grandma the proverbial boot? The answer lies somewhere in the web of issues and feelings woven together in this new relationship. To keep from calling for the ouster of your baby's grandparents, you may want to reflect on the following.

- How involved would both of you like the grandparents to be? Some couples so welcome the support and love grandparents provide that they are happy with daily visits and extended stays. These couples typically enjoy healthy relationships with their parents and in-laws long before baby arrives. Others have more difficult relationships with their parents or in-laws and function better with more privacy. It's also common for your relationship with parents and in-laws to change post-baby. After all, they will likely be more frequent guests and quite possibly more frequent advice-givers. You may end up needing more alone time than you predicted. Still, it's a good idea to begin the discussion of grandparent involvement now. As you discuss this, realize that your spouse's parents are very special and dear to your spouse, and they likely want to be close to their new grandbaby. That said, it is important that you honestly and tactfully discuss the issue of grandparent visits. To avoid hurt feelings and confusion later, iron out some of the specific post-birth issues now. For instance, will either set of grandparents be staying with you following the birth? Do you need to set up a rotation for grandparent houseguests? Are drop-ins OK, or do you prefer to schedule visits, at least with a pre-visit phone call? When grandparents are visiting, are you both comfortable asking them for help with various household/baby tasks that may be wearing you both out, or do you feel the need to treat them like guests?

- How do you handle advice? One of the wonderful things about grandparents is that they have been down this baby road and can provide you with invaluable tips and information. One of the less wonderful things about some grandparents is that they may overstep their boundaries, believing (and expressing) that they know much better than you how to raise your child. On which side will your baby's grandparents fall? Time will tell, but you may have a pretty good idea already. Either way, ask yourself and each other: How well do I accept advice, especially from my parents or in-laws? At this point, how gentle or overbearing are the future grandparents? What might be the best way to deal with overbearing grandparents full of criticism or unsolicited advice? Am I overly sensitive to well-intended advice?

- Have you come to terms with the fact that the two of you are ultimately in charge and responsible for your child's well-being? Some individuals have fallen into a habit of deferring to their parents on most life issues, and parenting issues will be no different. This is the time to discuss and reevaluate this approach. You and your spouse are the team with executive power over your child's upbringing. Grandparents and others can be consulted as desired, but in the end, each of you must view each other as having the final say. To act otherwise undermines not only your parenting but your very marriage. Imagine, for instance, that a couple researched and decided upon the "attachment parenting" approach, which involves a great deal of physical closeness and sensitivity to baby's needs. Imagine further that the husband comes home to his wife and mother-in-law and hears the baby screaming in her crib. "What's up?" he asks. "Mom said I was spoiling her by wearing her in the carrier and said she should learn to be alone for a while," the wife responds. Husband is shocked that their decision has been so summarily dismissed. He may understandably be resentful and even withdraw from parenting decisions in the future.

No doubt you will have some challenging moments dealing with both the newest member of the family and the older generation. Like so many marriage issues, if you can anticipate and discuss some of the possible challenges ahead of time, you can avoid some misunderstandings and conflicts. As you navigate this delicate terrain with your spouse, remember that one day, God willing, your dear child will grow up to have a life of his own, and you'll want to be a welcome part of it too.

Question for him

How do your views on child rearing differ or mirror those of your in-laws and parents?

Question for her

How do you envision the grandparents' involvement those first days postpartum/post-adoption? Share this vision with your husband, and ask for his input as well.

Question for both

What strengths do you see in each other as future parents? Make a commitment to focus on these strengths.

Prayer

Dear Lord, we seek to honor our parents in their new role as grandparents to our child. Please help us to nurture this relationship and make our home welcoming and inviting to them.

12. Emotional Reaction to Baby

For I am the LORD, your God,
who grasp your right hand;
It is I who say to you,
Do not fear, I will help you.

ISAIAH 41:13

At life's great milestones, we have some preconceived notions about how we should feel or react. Graduation should bring on nostalgia and excitement. Our wedding should summon feelings of romance and glee. And baby? Well, the only appropriate feeling is joy, we might figure, and if we or our spouse deviates from that, then something is terribly amiss.

Now for reality: Giving birth or adopting a child is the most awesome, overwhelming, miraculous event in anyone's life. Our reactions to the enormity of the occasion and the following weeks vary widely. We rarely experience just one emotion, and this occasion is no different. Along with joy and gratitude, parents commonly describe feeling apprehension, self-doubt, anxiety, fear, and even boredom.

When Tom and Anna were planning their international adoption, they both looked forward to holding their baby and feeling greater joy than they had ever known. Imagine their surprise when they became, as they called it, "hijacked" by grief for the losses their dear baby son was enduring—loss of his foster mother, his homeland, and everything he had ever known. "I loved him so much and wanted to take away all his grief, but I couldn't," Anna explained.

When Sarah gave birth to their son, she and husband,

Rob, returned home with him in a state of shock and fear. "We're not up to the challenge," Rob remembers thinking. "And I thought that since I had carried him for nine months, I would feel this overwhelming closeness immediately," confided Sarah. "In reality, I felt scared and so restricted, like I would never again have a normal life. I couldn't go out, my husband was at work, and it was all very different than I had envisioned. It's disconcerting to feel this way when you think you're supposed to feel elated." Sarah did some online research, and after learning about the baby blues, she described feeling "a sense of relief, like I was normal." Until that point, she was certain she was the only mom who felt anything other than bliss following her child's birth.

If we can open ourselves to the possibility of experiencing many (sometimes conflicting) emotions, we may deal more effectively with them and feel less "hijacked" by them. When we're caught totally off-guard, we can find ourselves thinking, "I shouldn't be feeling this way!" which allows unproductive guilt to creep in. As a sage grandmother once explained, "You feel how you feel, and that's OK." There is no one correct way to respond to this life-changing event.

What about when our spouse is feeling something very different than we are or is feeling something he or she is really not proud of? Can we accept that spouse's feelings without judgment and even help him or her come to terms with the experience? In the month following his son's birth, Eric turned to his wife, Terri, and blurted out a not-uncommon husband sentiment: "You know I love Eli. This has nothing to do with that, but I feel like I've lost you since you became a mother." At first Terri was peeved by his comment. She was giving motherhood her all. She was sleep-deprived and stressed. And now Eric was whining that she wasn't attentive to him when she was dealing with all of these new responsibilities? Luckily, she was actually too irritated to even respond, so Eric continued, "I know how hard you're working, and I'm not saying you're doing anything wrong. I just miss you. I'm almost jealous of the baby because he gets to be with you. I miss having time to talk to you, to go out with you." Even in her state of exhaustion, Terri began to listen and understand that Eric was sharing something difficult. Just having Terri listen made Eric feel he really hadn't lost his wife after all.

Lydia was a relaxed, easygoing woman. No one would ever describe her as tense or irritable—except her husband now that they had a baby. Lydia's overwhelming emotion after the baby was anxiety. Was the house clean enough for a baby? Was the baby nursing enough? Was she attentive enough? Would the baby get sick from the neighbor's sneezing?

For weeks, the outgrowth of this anxiety and worry was irritability and criticism of her husband, Joe. Lydia was so uncertain and anxious about her own parenting that she could find nothing but fault with Joe's parenting as well. Once in the middle of a tirade about how Joe had failed to properly clean a pacifier, she broke down. "I'm sorry," she said. "I had no idea I would be this anxious all the time and I'm taking it out on you. All I feel is tense anymore." Having Lydia explain the feelings behind her irritability made all the difference to Joe, who had been feeling like the worst husband and father for weeks. Now that they were honestly communicating, he could help her work on the anxiety and tension.

If there is one thread woven through all of the parenting/marriage issues we discuss, it is the importance of communication. When you struggle with varying feelings following your baby's arrival, try to gently and thoughtfully communicate your struggles to your spouse, and try to listen understandingly when your spouse exposes this vulnerable side.

Question for him

Can you recall a time that you shared your feelings with your wife? If so, share that memory with her.

Questions for her

Were you surprised by any of the emotions the couples said they felt? Why or why not?

Question for both

What emotions are you experiencing as you anticipate baby's arrival? Share those emotions with each other.

Prayer

Dear Lord, we are all complicated creatures. Although we will love and cherish and be forever grateful for our child, we know we will experience a variety of emotions as we adapt to our new roles. We pray that each morning we may rise with a feeling of joy and gratitude that we have been called to love and nurture one of your little ones. Amen.

13. Sleep

Come to me, all you who labor
and are burdened,
and I will give you rest.

MATTHEW 11:28

"Get all the rest you can now!" friends and family jokingly advise as baby's due date approaches.

"You think you're tired now," they warn when either of you discusses pregnancy-induced sleep disruptions, "just wait until the baby arrives!"

Such comments are irritating on so many levels. Just in case new parents-to-be aren't apprehensive enough, some people always seem to be waiting in the wings, ready to add to that anxiety.

As in so many off-handed comments, of course, there is a nugget of truth: Sleep deprivation can and often does hit new parents hard. Unfortunately, it's not really a laughing matter. Many of us can recall times when we pulled all-nighters for work or school. *It wasn't so bad,* we assure ourselves. *We're tough. We can deal with a little fatigue.*

Such thinking can be helpful in keeping our spirits up as we prepare for the challenge of parenting. However, it is important to keep in mind that the realities of sleep deprivation can be serious. Our bodies have physical limitations that we need to acknowledge and accept. Some research you may want to consider for your own physical, mental, and emotional well-being follows.

- Sleep difficulties are worst in the first month postpartum. This is something to remember if, after a couple of weeks of parenting, you begin to feel you will never sleep well again. It should get better.

- The longer new moms were awake at night, the more likely they were to have negative moods during the day.

- The more exhausted moms reported feeling, the worse their scores on a depression test.

- Improvements in children's sleep patterns have been associated with improvements in maternal depression.

In summary, research has substantiated that sleep deprivation is serious, affecting mood and sense of well-being. But what does this grim news mean for you? Is it just inevitable that we suffer serious consequences from fatigue?

Here are some tips you may find helpful:

- Be mindful of your physical limitations. There is no such thing as a supermom or superdad. Go easy on yourself. The early weeks and months of parenting are not the time to try to be an all-star at work or to keep an immaculate house. Rest whenever and however you can. Let the things nonessential to daily life slip—with no guilt!

- Accept help. Many of us have an independent streak that can border on pride. When friends offer to bring dinner or sit with the baby while you nap, graciously accept. They wouldn't have offered if they didn't want to help. If they are parents themselves, they are offering because they understand your exhaustion.

- Keep an eye on your spouse. Is he or she especially irritable and tense? Take a good look at each other. Can you see physical signs of fatigue? Encourage each other to make sleep a priority; encourage each other to nap or go to bed at night with chores undone. Babies take up so much time that we feel the need to work like crazy while they nap, even at the expense of much-needed sleep. Christine remembers being so tired that she put the baby down for a nap and stood in the kitchen crying for no apparent reason. David advised her to rest, which she didn't think she could do because she had "so many things to do." After lying on the couch, crying and thinking, "I'll never be able to rest," she quickly fell asleep. When she woke up an hour later, she felt like a new person. Without David's insistence, she would have tried to spend that hour "productively."

- When one spouse, usually mom, stays home in the early weeks to take care of the new baby, it's tempting for the other spouse to feel that she can do all nightly caregiving because she can sleep during the day while the baby sleeps. While she may be able to nap now and then, dads should realize that a good night's sleep is essential. She can't care for a baby all day if she never gets a decent night's sleep. Dad, pitch in a couple of nights a week, even if you have to put in long days at work. A couple of nights a week can make all the difference.

- On the other hand, it's also tempting to think that each parent has to be equally sleep-deprived. However, many couples find it helpful in the earliest days and weeks for mom and baby to sleep separately from dad, especially if baby is nursing. This way, at least one parent is well rested the next day and can tend to all the household tasks that need to be done while mom catnaps as she can. This arrangement also helps to stave off the bickering that often results from two sleep-deprived people. Dad can take the high road and say, "I will not be offended by that comment. You are tired. Let me tend to the baby while you rest a while." Couples with more than one child have said this arrangement allows dad the energy to tend to the older children while mom focuses on the constant caregiving a newborn requires.

Those early days of getting to know your little one are especially magical and exciting. You will look at that new child with more awe, wonder, and love than you can imagine. With some planning and attention to sleep issues, you will have the physical and emotional energy needed to savor this memorable era.

Questions for him

Given your unique situation, work out an initial plan for dealing with the sleep challenges of new baby care. Possible points to consider: Will you take turns getting up in the night? Will mom and baby sleep separately? What can be left "undone" around the house to gain more time for rest? On whom can you call if you both need some extra help? Keep in mind that this plan can be altered as needed.

Questions for her

How do you best unwind at the end of the day? How can you help your spouse carve out time for this?

Question for both

Saint Paul tells us that love is patient and kind. (See 1 Corinthians 13.) How might this Scripture relate to this section?

Prayer

Father, we come to you as new parents who want to support and love each other during this beautiful, exciting, and demanding era of our lives. Please guide us and provide us with wisdom, patience, and understanding as we care for each other and our new child. Amen.

14. Saints

The smoke of the incense along with the prayers of the holy ones went up before God from the hand of the angel.

As Catholics, the communion of saints should never be too far from our thoughts. These honored members of our Church are role models for us as well as prayer partners. We can call upon them for prayers at any time. As we look forward to our newest and most important vocation, let's take a look at some of the saints who are waiting to be called on.

Saint Agnes Le Thi Thanh (1781–1841), martyr: The mother of six children, Saint Agnes was tortured to death for her faith. Throughout days of savage beatings, she prayed to the Blessed Mother for strength and said that due to the Blessed Mother's intercession, she felt no pain. Saint Agnes's reliance on the Blessed Mother's intercession could inspire moms fearing the pain of childbirth.

Saint Bernadette Soubirous (1844–1879), patron of illness, poverty, those ridiculed for their piety: As a young girl, Bernadette was visited by the Blessed Mother in Lourdes, France. On one occasion, the Blessed Mother told her to dig in the ground to find a spring, which she did. Today, pilgrims the world over visit Lourdes to seek healing in the water of the spring. Bernadette is a wonderful saint to turn to in times of illness in your family.

Saint Elizabeth Ann Seton (1774–1821), patron of widows and those ridiculed for their faith and against the death of children and parents: Elizabeth Ann Seton is a great saint to turn to when you feel stressed beyond your limits. After all, she was left widowed with five young children at the age of twenty-eight! After her husband's death, she converted to Catholicism in an anti-Catholic young America, founded the first religious congregation of women in the United States, the first Catholic American orphanage and free Catholic day school. When you need to achieve the impossible, call on Saint Elizabeth.

Saint Gianna Molla (1922–1962), patron of mothers and physicians: Saint Gianna lost her life shortly after the birth of her third child. During her pregnancy, she was found to have a uterine tumor and advised to abort the baby, which she refused to do. Ask Saint Gianna to pray for mom and doctor throughout pregnancy. After baby is born, you both may have days when you feel a little "sacrificed out" by your parental duties. Turn to Saint Gianna for prayers and reflect on the sacrifice she made for her baby daughter.

Saint Rita of Cascia (1381–1457), patron of difficult marriages, impossible causes, infertility, and parenthood: Saint Rita endured great sorrows in her vocation as wife and mother, first dealing with a very difficult husband, then becoming a widow at a young age, and losing both of her sons. All marriages and families will go through rough patches, and Saint Rita is an excellent prayer partner for those parents facing difficult times.

Saint Thomas More (1478–1535), patron of lawyers: Widely respected statesman of England and father of four, Saint Thomas More was executed for holding fast to Church teaching rather than giving in to political pressure. As a parent, no doubt you wish to be a strong example of honor, courage, and faithfulness to your children. Martyr Saint Thomas More is a great role model and intercessor.

Saint Veronica (first century): The patron saint of photographers and laundry workers, Saint Veronica is depicted in the sixth Station of the Cross. Tradition holds that Veronica came forward to provide the only comfort she could to the suffering Jesus: she simply wiped his face. As a parent, you will be endlessly providing small acts of comfort. When you start to lose sight of the beauty of this vocation, ask Saint Veronica to pray for you.

Blessed Louis Martin (1823–1894): The gentle, devout father of the much-beloved Saint Thérèse of Lisieux. The letters of his wife and Thérèse testify to his affectionate, loving, and tender nature. Left a widower to raise his five surviving children, Blessed Louis is the ideal prayer partner for parents seeking both strength and gentleness.

Saint Joseph, foster father of Jesus: The patron of fathers, workers, unborn children, immigrants, against doubt, and for a happy death: Of all the men of the time, Saint Joseph was chosen to be the earthly father and the daily role model for Jesus. Parents-to-be, you have likewise been chosen to guide and love your children while they are on earth so that they may grow up to glorify the Father they have in heaven. Saint Joseph is a great prayer partner in child rearing.

Blessed Mother, the Queen of all Saints: Fearing labor and delivery? Mary understands; she was a young girl giving birth in a stable. Have a suffering child? Mary understands; she stood by Jesus as he was crucified. Experiencing great joy and awe at the gift of parenthood? Mary understands; her *Magnificat* captures our joy. For any parenting issue, the Blessed Mother stands ready to pray.

Question for him

In addition to these saints, who among your friends and family can you count on for prayers as you enter the vocation of fatherhood?

Question for her

In addition to these saints, who among your friends and family can you count on for prayers as you enter the vocation of motherhood?

Questions for both

Which of these saints do you think you will most frequently call on for prayers? Which ones inspire you by their life of faith? Are you familiar with other saints you would like to tell your spouse about?

Prayer

Dear Lord, we thank you for the communion of saints. We thank you for faithful friends who pray for us. Please make us ever mindful of our need for prayer and our need to pray for others. Amen.

Acknowledgments

Crawford, M. (2007). *When Two Become Three: Nurturing Your Marriage After Baby Arrives*. Grand Rapids, MI: Revell.

Harvard Medical School (2011). "Beyond the 'Baby Blues.'" Harvard Mental Health Letter, 28(3), 1–3.

Houts, R., Barnett-Walker, K., Paley, B., & Cox, M. (2008). "Patterns of Couple Interaction During the Transition to Parenthood," 15(1), 103–122.

Meijer, A. & van den Wittenboer, G. (2007). "Contribution of Infants' Sleep and Crying to Marital Relationship of First-time Parent Couples in the First Year After Childbirth." *Journal of Family Psychology*, 21(1), 49–57.

Moller, K., Hwang, P., Wickbert, B. (2008). "Couple Relationship and Transition to Parenthood: Does Workload at Home Matter? *Journal of Reproductive and Infant Psychology*, 26(1), 57–68.

Olsson, A., Lundqvist, M., Faxelid, E., Nissen, E. (2005). "Women's Thoughts About Sexual Life After Childbirth: Focus Group Discussions With Women After Childbirth." *Scandinavian Journal of Caring Sciences*, 19(4), 381–387.

Olsson, A., Robertson, E., Bjorklund, A., Nissen, E. (2010). "Fatherhood in Focus, Sexual Activity Can Wait: New Fathers' Experience About Sexual Life After Childbirth." *Scandinavian Journal of Caring Sciences*, 24(4), 716–725.

Papalia, D., Olds, S., Feldman, R. (2011). *Human Development*. New York, New York.

Ross, L., Murray, B., Steiner, M. (2005). "Sleep and Perinatal Mood Disorders: A Critical Review." *Journal of Psychiatry & Neuroscience*, 30(4), 247–256.

Shapiro, A., Gottman, J., and Carrere, S. (2000). "The Baby and the Marriage: Identifying Factors That Buffer Against Decline in Marital Satisfaction After the First Baby Arrives." *Journal of Family Psychology*, 14(1), 59–70.